The Dictionary According to Mommy

The Dictionary According to Mommy

Joyce Armor

Illustrations by
Christine Tripp

Meadowbrook Press

Distributed by Simon & Schuster
New York

Library of Congress Cataloging-in-Publication Data

Armor, Joyce.
The dictionary according to mommy / by Joyce Armor.
p. cm.
1. Mothers—Humor. 2 Pregnancy—Humor.
3. Children—Humor.
I. Title.
PN6231.M68A76 1989 818'.5402—dc19
88-36449
ISBN 0-88166-162-7

Editor: Bruce Lansky
Production Editor: Sandy McCullough
Art Director: Maria Mazzara
Production Manager: Pam Scheunemann
Illustrated by Christine Tripp

Simon & Schuster Ordering #: 0-671-68384-5

Published by Meadowbrook Press, 18318 Minnetonka Boulevard, Deephaven, MN 55391.

BOOK TRADE DISTRIBUTION by Simon & Schuster, a division of Simon and Schuster, Inc., 1230 Avenue of the Americas, New York, NY 10020.

89 90 91 92 5 4 3 2

Printed in the United States of America.

To Mom—
Now I understand

Acknowledgments

Many thanks to Bruce Lansky, an editor with the devious mind of a mother; my sister and friend, Gail; and all the other mothers who let me use their amusing and/or miserable experiences for my own personal gain.

Introduction

The real reason children are on this earth is to turn their mothers' hair gray. That's a given. They get into life-and-death struggles over three stale Cheerios®, act their worst when your mother-in-law is around to take notes, and spend naptime dreaming of ways to avoid going to bed that evening. They thrive on two hours of sleep a night, could teach the most experienced burglar how to break into whatever it is you most want them to stay out of, and find new ways each day to make you spend money.

All you have to do in return is clothe, feed, bathe, and educate them; teach them morals and values; foster their hopes and dreams; nurture their wounds, spirits, and self-esteem; instill them with a sense of responsibility and abiding faith; and love them unconditionally.

There are a few things that will get you through the experience, and in fact give you the better end of the deal. For instance, when your child puts his little arms around you and says, "I love you sooooo much, Mommy," wiping away all his previous sins. Or when you observe the joy, wonder, and innocence of childhood; realize children are the hope for the future; and know the world will be all right if you do your best. Also important is maintaining both perspective and a sense of humor. If this book makes you laugh or remember a horrifying stage of child development fondly, the hours I spent trying to write it with my two-year-old on my back yelling, "Type a B, Mommy, type a B!" while my four-year-old ransacked the house will have been worth it. But if all else fails, you can always call your hairdresser and at least get rid of the gray.

Joyce Armor

adolescence The stage of growth that turns a perfectly normal child into an alien.

afterbirth When the hard part begins.

afterpains A chance to relive the highlights of your labor.

air force The strength you'll need to blow up balloons until your children grow older and think balloons are uncool.

allowance The weekly bribe that's never as much as the other kids get.

amnesia The condition that enables a woman who has gone through labor to have sex again.

amniocentesis Seedling needling.

anesthetic The painkiller that crazy women refuse during labor.

angel The sleeping child you thought was the Bad Seed when she was awake.

anxiety How Mommy uses up her extra adrenaline.

armed force The amount of strength it takes for a boy to make rude noises with his armpit.

autoharp Lecturing the children while you're driving them to school.

babbling The language mothers are reduced to by the end of a particularly difficult day.

baby book Where you put locks of the baby's hair and pictures of him naked so you can embarrass him when he's a teenager.

baby diet A weight-loss method for moms that involves countless meal interruptions.

baby food The mushy sludge it's your job to convince the baby she likes.

baby proof To remove from your home dangers to the baby such as electrical cords, poisons, siblings, etc.

baby shower What you get when you change a diaper too slowly.

baby-sitter A teenager who will eat your food and watch your TV for money unless she gets a last-minute date.

baby swing A safe place to put the baby unless she has a brother.

baby talk The language adults use that makes babies spit up.

baby toys What was once in those empty boxes babies love to play with.

backstroke The move a 7th-grade boy makes to see if a girl is wearing a bra.

bananas What babies prefer to clay.

Band-Aid® The owie remedy that makes a child stop crying almost as fast as if you put it over her mouth.

bangs The first thing a child hacks off when she learns to use scissors.

bathroom Where your child doesn't need to go until you're backing your car out of the driveway.

battery operated Able to create loud noises that make Mommy and Daddy crazy.

bed The padded trampoline where children do their imitation of the Flying Wallendas.

bilingual A child who can ignore parents in two languages.

biology What makes boys say "vroom" without ever being taught when they push toy cars.

birth certificate Irrefutable proof that the child who seems to be from another planet is really yours.

birth control Not going berserk during labor.

birthing chair What polite doctors offer to women in labor.

biting What dogs do to children, children do to other children, and mothers do to their fingernails.

bladder The only part of Mommy that Baby flattens like a pancake during the last few weeks of pregnancy.

blankie That deteriorating gray rag you can't coax, bribe, or strong-arm away from your toddler.

bonding The closeness forged with newborns that later helps parents forgive teenagers for acting like teenagers.

bonk The sound parents dread once their children reach swing height.

bookmark The welt raised when one child clobbers another with the hardcover edition of *The Cat in the Hat.*

books Literary works that entertained children before television was invented.

bottle-feeding An opportunity for Daddy to get up at 2:00 A.M., too.

boyfriend The hoodlum your daughter is going to marry someday over your dead body.

braces What you pay a fortune to hear your child complain about.

brain drain Trying to remember the vitally important topic you were discussing before the children interrupted.

breast pump The device that sucks gallons of milk from your friend's breasts and a drop-and-a-half from yours.

breech birth Rear entry.

brotherly love The philosophy that no one can beat up on your siblings but you.

brother/sister A combination punching bag and best friend.

bubbles What your child blows six of before he spills the rest of the bottle.

bumper pads Cushioned barriers that keep babies from chewing their way out of their cribs.

burping The habit that is cute when babies do it and disgusting when their fathers do it.

call girl A teenager who spends more time on the phone than an AT&T operator.

car seat Where a ten-minute nap is enough to keep the baby awake for the next twelve hours.

cartoons What your husband uses the children as an excuse to watch.

catheter A bladder siphon that allows hospital employees and other strangers to examine your urine close up.

cesarean section A surgical method of delivery used in emergencies such as fetal distress or when the doctor's next car payment is due.

channeling Flipping through the TV channels so quickly that the kids don't notice the children's special that conflicts with your favorite show.

chastity belt A labor-saving device.

childproof A pill bottle that you need a pipe wrench to open.

circumcision Surgery that makes a baby's penis look like the penis of his father, who had the same surgery for the same reason.

colic A nonspecific cause of fussiness in babies that makes new parents remember to use birth control.

college The education you want for your kids but need to win the lottery to pay for.

common knowledge What everyone on the face of the earth but you knows about breastfeeding.

computers The high-tech machines that enable first graders to make their parents feel like morons.

constipation Nature's way of making pregnant women practice pushing.

contagious The kind of disease you find out your child has a day after he's exposed all his friends and relatives.

contraception What many mommies know is not as infallible as the Pope.

contractions What are to cramps as Lake Michigan is to a puddle.

cradle Where you can't put a baby unless she's an only child.

cradle cap What bald babies wear so they don't look like Telly Savalas.

cravings An excuse to gluttonize your way through pregnancy.

crawling baby Mother Nature's vacuum cleaner.

crib Where you put the baby so you can check on her every three minutes to make sure she's still breathing.

crying The weeping and wailing that occurs for the first few years—or until you learn to control your outbursts.

cycle The type of canned dog food most crawling babies prefer.

cynic A person who believes children give us high blood pressure on purpose.

daily double Buying two of everything so your children won't kill each other.

danger zone The area surrounding an undiapered baby.

dark ages Those dismal days before disposable diapers were invented.

deadweight A corollary to the law of gravity that states that a sleeping child weighs three times as much as the same child at any other time.

debriefing When a toddler removes his diaper soon after you've put it on.

defense What you'd better have around de yard if you're going to let de children outside.

déjà vu When you respond to your child the same way your mother responded to you.

dentist The sadist you pretend not to be afraid of for the children's sake.

diaper rash A boo-boo you'd rather not fix with a kiss.

dilation One of those things a pregnant woman has to take her doctor's word for.

dining room The distance you put between plates at mealtime so your children won't snatch each other's food.

disposable diapers Your opportunity to make a personal contribution to the waste disposal industry.

double fault When both your children are guilty.

DPT shots The injections you're glad the baby is too young to remember you made him get.

dress code The unwritten law that teenagers must dress alike to assert their independence.

drooling How teething babies wash their chins.

drums What your child gets on his birthday from relatives who hate you.

due date What only *seems* light-years away.

dumbwaiter One who asks if the kids would care to order dessert.

dust bowl Your once-beautiful lawn by the time the kids go back to school in September.

ear infection An opportunity to wrestle your baby to the floor and cram an antibiotic down his throat.

eating for two A nice way to say "pigging out."

eat one's words What any person who has ever said "I'll never bribe my children with food" must do.

educational toys Colorful, stimulating, and expensive playthings that parents like more than babies do.

elastiphobia Fear of making it into the *Guinness Book of World Records* for "Most Stretch Marks."

embarrassment Taking your preschooler out in public when she's wearing an outfit *she* picked out.

embryo A new acorn on the family tree.

energy What children still have a half tank of when parents are on empty.

episiotomy Cutting a wide birth.

equations The point at which you need a tutor to explain your child's math homework to you.

even-tempered Able to appear calm when you discover your daughter playing "doctor" with the neighbor boy.

extended family One that can't get any more credit.

face-lift What the baby gives you when she gets a vice-like grip on a clump of your hair.

fads The reason your child's jeans cost twice as much as yours.

false labor All stressed up and nowhere to go.

falsies The little lies you tell your child like "You can't ride the horsey in front of K-Mart because it's broken."

family bed One of the cheaper methods of birth control.

family planning The art of spacing your children the proper distance apart to keep you on the edge of financial disaster.

fantasy Imagining your children picking up their toys gleefully and thanking you for the privilege.

fast food Unwanted portions of Baby's meals that become projected missiles.

father The guy who says, "C'mere honey, I think his diaper needs changing."

favorite son The one who brownnoses better on any given day.

feedback The inevitable result when Baby doesn't like his strained carrots.

feeding schedule What Baby is on until Mommy tries to make plans around it.

feet of clay What Mommy ends up with after the children leave the Play Doh® on the floor.

fertility A condition that varies inversely with your bank account.

fever What your child comes down with the day before you leave on vacation.

fifth dimension Where all those missing pieces of puzzles, Lincoln Logs,® and Mr. Potatohead® are.

fingernails Where children store their dirt collections.

first trimester The first three months of pregnancy when you wonder, "Is it too late to hire a surrogate mother?"

fish out of water What you get when you let the cat or the baby too close to the aquarium.

flattop A girl who hasn't begun to mature yet.

flaws Those irritating characteristics that make your children most like you.

floor What supports the decomposing mound of clothes and toys in your child's bedroom.

foot-dragging A child's method of ruining new shoes before the check you bought them with clears.

forceps Giant baby tweezers.

frisk Checking all pockets for bugs, toads, and snakes before letting your boys back into the house.

froosh The sound of Rice Krispies® being ground into the carpet.

full name What you call your child when you're mad at him.

game warden An adult who breaks up Candyland® and Monopoly® fights.

geezer How your children perceive you, no matter how hip *you* think you are.

general admission When a child confesses guilt but won't give any details.

genes The reason your daughter will grow up to blame her thighs on you.

get lost What you'd like your kids to do until it really happens.

give up To let your children run amok.

glare A look teenagers use to insult their parents without saying anything they could get punished for.

gloat What you do when the neighbor's child prodigy wets her pants.

golden rule Take good care of your children now so you can sponge off them when you're old and wrinkly.

grades What we're lucky kids get and parents don't.

grandparents The people who think your children are wonderful even though they're sure you're not raising them right.

grasp reflex The reaction of a new father when he sees a new mother's boobs.

gravity Why parts of your body are getting closer to your children.

gray matter Those streaks in your hair that you can thank your children for.

grenade What it looks like someone lobbed in your window on the days you spend "quality time" with the children.

growth chart The record that proves your baby is actually getting taller as she's getting heavier.

guardian angels The only rational explanation for how children survive to adulthood.

guesswork Trying to figure out what kind of shriveled rodent just went through the washer and dryer in your son's pocket.

guilt A major occupational hazard of motherhood.

gumshoe Your child's Bazooka,® your Reebok.®

haircut A chance for everyone at the beauty salon to hear just how loud your toddler can cry.

hairstyle That bizarre thing on your teenager's head.

Halloween The holiday for which you get to spend ninety hours making a costume so your child can wear it once.

hand-me-downs Clothes that teenagers would rather die than get from siblings but love to buy at second-hand stores.

handwriting on the wall Early penmanship efforts that make Mommy hyperventilate.

hard labor A redundancy, like "working mother."

harlot Any woman who flirts with a pregnant woman's husband.

harmonica The toy that teaches children to make music while drooling.

hearing aid A child who informs you of all the rotten things her brother says when you're out of earshot.

hearsay What toddlers do when anyone mutters a dirty word.

heartburn Nature's way of reminding pregnant women that unborn babies don't like their cuisine too spicy.

heirlooms The family keepsakes you're saving for your children, who aren't allowed to see or touch them.

heredity Grounds for blaming your child's faults on the in-laws.

hero worship The reason your daughter is dressing like Hulk Hogan.

high chair Where you put the baby when you want to know where he'll be for the next ten minutes.

holes What young children won't wear jeans with and teenagers won't wear jeans without.

home pregnancy test A chance to panic sooner.

homework What teaches children how to get things done at the last minute.

hootenannies If you remember them, you're too old to get pregnant.

hormones The little critters that make pregnant women act demented.

hose down What toilet-trained little boys do to the bathroom.

hospital The last place Mommy will get to rest until the next time she gives birth.

hospital gown An embarrassing garment that hospitals make mothers in labor wear to discourage them from going out for pizza.

hospital tour A chance to see all the hospital facilities you won't give a hoot about when you're in labor.

ice cream truck The only thing that will get your couch potatoes to move.

idealist A mother who thinks hers is the one child who won't go through the Terrible Two's.

immature Anyone who argues with a two-year-old (and loses).

immediate gratification A parent's desire for instant obedience, which it is a child's job to thwart.

immediately In the little twerp's own good time.

impregnable A woman whose memory of labor is still vivid.

independent How we want our children to be as long as they do everything we say.

induction Forced labor.

ineptitude What babies have come to expect in new parents.

infant Crib jockey.

ingrate Every child until he becomes a parent.

inside out Children's clothing in its normal state.

instant replay When the little bugger does what you just told him to cease and desist.

intercourse What's much easier to do than to explain to children.

introvert A child you're sure is plotting to overthrow the government.

jam-packed Any PB & J sandwich a child makes.

jealousy Why your lap must be big enough to hold more than one child.

jet lag A condition mothers fall victim to without ever leaving home.

job Where adults get to communicate with other adults and are actually paid for their work.

joint resolution A parental agreement not to let the children smoke marijuana.

jumping-off place Any piece of furniture above floor level.

just desserts What every child would eat if he could plan the menu.

juvenile delinquency The future you envision for your child the first time he sneaks a cookie without asking.

kamikaze A child, a trike, a hill.

kickback A self-defense technique that most children master by the age of 18 months.

killjoy Someone who suggests you wear your old jeans too soon after childbirth.

kindergarten What you can't wait for your child to start until he does.

kiss Boo-booectomy.

kook A child who eats beets without being threatened.

labor camp Where women who can't stop retelling their labor stories should be sent.

labor coach The person who reminds you to breathe during labor.

labor day A holiday celebrated by women who are done having children.

lampshades What babies and drunks like to wear on their heads.

lap pad What protects your legs while the baby burps on other parts of your body.

large scale What you need in the ninth month of pregnancy.

last straw The one your children will fight to the death over.

layette Baby trousseau.

laying on of hands A method of discipline some parents use when sermons don't work.

lead by the nose A last-ditch method for getting your child to go with you.

leakproof Diapers that weren't tested on your baby.

leapfrog The game that allows a brother to "accidentally" crush his sister's head.

leashes The restraints you think other parents are horrible to use until you have children of your own.

likely story Any excuse that involves giant monsters.

little dipper A child who sticks his fingers in his milk glass.

long line What you're in the middle of when your son says he feels like he might throw up.

"look out!" What it's too late for your child to do by the time you scream it.

lullaby The off-key melody your baby avoids listening to by falling asleep.

lunch counter A child who makes sure he has the identical number of grapes, crackers, and Cheerios® as his siblings.

macho The genetic defect that makes men want to teach toddlers to box.

magic carpet One that doesn't show apple juice, chocolate pudding, or pizza stains.

make believe To pretend to agree that your friend's baby is cuter than the babies in the diaper commercials.

mama What the baby learns to say after dada, bye-bye, and a hundred other words.

man in the street What a pregnant woman's husband will be if he makes "fat" jokes.

manipulation What usually works better than strength in dealing with children.

manual dexterity Your ability to reach the wipes while still keeping a baby with an open diaper pinned to the changing table.

masculine Unable to cope with dirty diapers.

mask of pregnancy The disguise a pregnant woman wears if she gains too much weight.

materialistic Parents who get upset when their children set fire to the sofa.

maternal Pretending to need help when you're making cookies.

maternity clothes What a pregnant woman wears to show people there's a reason she's fat.

mature Parents who can admit they don't know what they're doing.

meltdown Your reward for letting the children leave crayons in the car.

milestone The moment you stop worrying about something hurting the baby and start worrying about the baby hurting something.

milk run The path spilled milk takes off the side of the table to the floor.

miracle 1. The birth of a baby. **2.** The fact that you lived to tell about it.

misconception A pregnancy that begins while using birth control.

modesty What women in labor soon get over.

moment of truth When your child wants to know how the stork got the baby inside your tummy.

mommyitis The over-attachment that makes Baby cry hysterically when Mommy leaves to go to the bathroom.

moral code The high principles you are determined to instill in your children, even if you have to lie, cheat, or steal to do it.

morning sickness An opportunity to see if the inside of your toilet bowl is really clean.

mother superior The concept mothers try to sell their two-year-olds.

mother's weight None of your damn business.

motorcycles Exciting vehicles mothers won't let their children or husbands buy.

nanoseconds What a small child's attention span is measured in.

nap time When Mommy cleans up the morning mess while the children rest up to make the afternoon mess.

natural gas Yet another nagging symptom of pregnancy.

neighborly Willing to baby-sit on short notice.

nesting instinct A burning desire to dust your baseboards and polish your appliances before the baby is born.

night-light A safety device that allows you just enough light to see what you tripped over.

night terrors Frightening episodes during which new mothers dream they're pregnant again.

nobody The person who's responsible for leaving the refrigerator door open, scratching the furniture, and shaving the cat.

nocturnal emissions Dirty diapers in the middle of the night.

noise What there's too much of when the kids are home and not enough of when they're gone.

no-no The first two-syllable word your child learns to say.

normal Unlike your children.

nose The olfactory organ you stop breathing through the day you start changing diapers.

noses, runny Why parents should buy tissues by the gross.

nothing The answer to "What did you do in school today?"

nurse The only person who truly cares about a new mother's bowel movements.

nursing bra A brassiere that takes over feeding the baby when Mommy's too tired.

nutritious The food you make your children eat before they're allowed to eat the food they like.

obedience A trait that is alien to the human child.

obstetrician The doctor who tells you you're doing fine when you think you're caught in the jaws of death.

occupant The name on the mail you tell your child is addressed to him.

on the wagon Where three children want to be when the wagon only holds one.

open-and-shut What children can only do half of when it comes to doors.

open-door policy The reason flies can come and go as they please in any house where children live.

opinionated Anyone who knows more than you do about child care.

outdoors Where children gather mud and debris to bring indoors.

overhang The abdominal condition that tells new mothers it's time to buy the Jane Fonda workout tapes.

ow The first word spoken by children with older siblings.

pacifier What would work much better if it could be glued to the baby's face.

pacifist A child who will fight if you try to take his pacifier away.

pajama party When teenage friends get together overnight and talk about the friends who aren't there.

pantyhose What your three-year-old son enjoys wearing more than you do.

paradox Two obstetricians.

park Where the children play while you scan the area for psychopaths.

pediatrician The doctor who treats Mommy's anxiety attacks.

pelvic exam One test you can't cheat on.

phase The difficult stage your child moves into while you're still recovering from the last one.

piggy bank The place you hide coins so the baby can't eat them.

pig latin The language you use for secrets until the kids are old enough to catch on.

pinch-hit A child's reflex action when someone snatches a toy from him.

playing dumb Pretending not to notice your children are misbehaving so you don't have to deal with it.

playpen Where you put the baby when she starts eating the plants.

playroom An enclosed area of the house you concede to the children.

poetic justice When your friend who had a pleasant pregnancy and easy delivery has a colicky baby.

population control Why God makes new parents too tired to have sex.

postpartum depression Your body's revenge for putting it through pregnancy.

preconceive To get pregnant before you intended to.

pregnant pause The amount of time it takes for a nine-months-pregnant woman to get out of a chair.

premature birth One that occurs before the expectant parents are well traveled and filthy rich.

prenatal When your life was still your own.

prepared childbirth A contradiction in terms.

preschool Where children learn how to spit, talk dirty, and bring home communicable diseases.

preshrunk A garment that will fit the baby for at least a week.

press release What parents want to issue the first time their child uses the toilet for the right purpose.

privacy What childless or very old couples have.

protective coloring When you color with your child to make sure she keeps her crayons on the book.

psychological warfare What the Pentagon could learn a lot about from toddlers.

puberty The stage children reach that makes parents start worrying about pregnancy all over again.

puddle A small body of water that draws other small bodies wearing dry shoes into it.

punctual Childless.

puppy love Why babies allow doggies to French-kiss them.

pushing The final effort to get a ten-pound baby through an opening the size of a dime.

rationalize To wait to get back into shape until after your last child is born.

rearrange What siblings do to each other's faces when parents aren't looking.

recessive genes The ones responsible for making the baby look like the offspring of your plumber.

relatives People you wish lived nearby so they could baby-sit on long week-ends.

remote control The TV-switching device invented by a nursing mother.

rest assured What you finally get when you have grown children.

revenge "Forgetting" to take the pill after your husband refuses to discuss the possibility of having more children.

reversible Dirty on both sides.

rhythm method Baby roulette.

rocking chair What a new mother puts more miles on than the family car.

rolling over A parent-pleasing trick babies pick up from dogs.

rude awakening When you're jolted from sleep by those dreaded words: "I wet my bed."

rugged individualism The characteristic we admire in adults and hate in children.

running mate A husband who discovers before his wife does that the baby has a dirty diaper.

safecracker One that doesn't have anybody's cooties on it.

sandbox The children's play area that the kids use almost as much as the neighborhood cats do.

saturation point What a diaper usually reaches before you reach the diaper.

school-age Old enough to know better.

scrapbook Where you put thousands of photos of your firstborn and a snapshot or two of your lastborn.

search warrant What you must have to enter a teenager's room.

seat belts Another form of child discipline, also known as spanking.

second-story man A daddy who reads two books to the kids at bedtime.

second trimester The second three months of pregnancy when you ask the question, "Will my husband notice if I eat this gallon of ice cream and side of beef before he gets home?"

secret What you tell the *National Enquirer* or a toddler if you want the news spread.

sensitive Able to commiserate over the death of a frog.

sentimental Unable to dispose of the baby's first fingernail clippings.

separatist A teenager who would rather die than be seen with his parents.

setting an example Hiding your sinful behavior from your children.

"settle down!" An abstract command ignored by children through the ages.

sex drive When you go for a ride in the car to fool around because there's no privacy at home.

sharing What children only do when parents are watching.

shatterproof An item that hasn't come in contact with a three year old.

shopping cart Where you can fit children or groceries, but not both.

shortcoming What can still get you pregnant.

shortfall An accident you don't need your medical insurance for.

show-and-tell When children share their gerbils, tonsils, and sisters' toys with classmates.

show-off A child who is more talented than yours.

sibling rivalry The reason you must search the house periodically for concealed weapons.

sickness What keeps kids in bed all week, until Saturday morning.

sleep What only fathers and bed wetters do soundly.

sleeping bag The haggard mother who has been up most of the night with the baby.

sleepover When a teenager spends the night at the home of a friend who has a later curfew.

slide The child's play apparatus that eighteen-month-olds can get up but not down.

slush fund The money children set aside to buy snow cones.

snail's pace What is infinitely faster than a preschooler dressing herself.

social outcast A school-age boy who admits he likes his sister.

soft soap What you find when you finally locate the Ivory® on the bottom of the bathtub.

soft spot A squishy area on the baby's head that corresponds to the one in your heart.

"some assembly required" Every father's nightmare.

soprano A boy whose private parts have gotten caught in his pants zipper.

sound barrier What is broken at least once at every child's birthday party.

spare time What women with no children have.

sperm The silver orb in the pinball game of procreation.

spinach The vegetable even Popeye couldn't make kids eat.

spinsterhood The life-style mothers of small children occasionally think of wistfully.

spit shine To wash your baby's face with the only liquid available.

spit-up Why you'd better get dressed for the party *after* you've burped the baby.

spoilsport Competition to see which grandparent can overindulge your children the most.

spunk One of those traits that is cuter in other people's children than in your own.

squeaky clean A condition that lasts approximately three minutes after a child's bath.

stage 1 labor When you still think it's fun.

stage 2 labor When you want to send your husband to Tijuana for illegal drugs.

stampede Why it's illegal to yell "Who wants ice cream?" in a room crowded with children.

standard deviation The reason your child's bizarre behavior is considered normal.

steeplechase The race to get the kids into the car and to church on time.

stereo The device teenagers use for their experiments on how many decibels it takes to reach the pain level.

sterilize What you do to your first baby's pacifier by boiling and to your last baby's pacifier by blowing on it.

storeroom The distance required between the supermarket aisles so that children in shopping carts can't quite reach anything.

straight flush When a child flushes the toilet without using it.

stretch marks Pregnancy service stripes.

stroller A moving vehicle from which the baby grabs bushes, parked cars, and stray dogs.

sugar daddy A father who lets the kids eat junk food when Mom's not around.

Super Bowl The occasion when children learn never to walk between Daddy's chair and the TV set.

Supermom Faster than a speeding spoonful of oatmeal, more powerful than a stubborn two-year-old, and able to leap tall piles of dirty clothes in a single bound.

supreme court Where sibling disputes still couldn't be resolved.

sweetbread The sugar sandwich your child makes if you let him fix his own lunch.

swimming pools What children often confuse with a restroom.

talent scout The person who doesn't want to hear from you the first time your baby smiles.

talent search Signing your kid up for dancing, soccer, gymnastics, and swimming lessons until you can find something she can do.

talking What you worry that your child will never start, and then that she'll never stop.

tattle To tell your husband the rotten things the kids did while he was out.

tax-deductible One of your child's most redeeming qualities.

teacher The recipient of all those unwanted health foods parents put in children's lunch boxes.

tear gas The only surefire method of getting children away from the television set.

teasing The trait boys have an extra gene for.

teething **1.** What you tell people your baby is doing when he cries. **2.** How nursing mothers decide it's time to wean their babies.

telephone What Mommy talks on while Baby defoliates the house plants.

temper tantrums What you should keep to a minimum so as not to upset the children.

terrible twos Your breasts if the baby quits nursing cold turkey.

textbook The kind of pregnancy other women have.

thesaurus Where you can find substitutes for those dirty words you used before you became a parent and had to be a good influence.

third trimester The third three months of pregnancy when you wonder, "How much longer can I keep from waddling?"

throwing up Grossing Mommy out and making her feel sorry for you at the same time.

thud The noise that is almost always followed by crying.

thunderstorm A chance to see how many family members can fit in one bed.

time What you had too much of before you became a mother and not enough of after.

time flies The reason your child will be wearing diapers one day and a purple mohawk the next.

time lag The delay between when a child falls down and when he starts to cry.

time out When Mommy retreats to her room until she can be nicer.

time warp What teenagers think their parents are caught in.

tinsel What mothers vacuum up from December to April, when they start vacuuming up Easter basket grass.

toehold One way to keep the baby still while you put his socks on.

toilet training When children teach their parents they'll use the toilet in their own good time, and not before.

toilet water What toddlers would rather play in than bath water.

tomorrow When you say you'll do those things the kids kept you from doing yesterday.

tooth fairy The little sprite who pays more for teeth left under pillows at Grandma's house than for teeth left under pillows at home.

toothpaste What young children swallow more of than vegetables.

top bunk Where you should never put a child wearing Superman jammies.

town crier A child who finds a reason to burst into tears every time you take him out in public.

tranquility A sleeping baby, a good book, and a tubal ligation.

transition The period of labor that bridges the gap between maintaining nicely and wanting to maim someone.

tug-of-war A game two children play by grappling over a toy neither of them would want if the other one didn't want it.

turncoat A baby who smiles and waves when you leave, but cries hysterically when the baby-sitter goes.

twilight sleep That time when you try to convince yourself the baby will stop crying before you have to get up.

twins Womb-mates.

twist and shout Maneuvers one-year-olds perform while getting their diapers changed.

two-minute warning When the baby's face turns red and she begins to grunt.

ultrasound The noise a crying baby makes.

umbilical cord The cord connecting baby to mother that becomes invisible after birth.

unarmed A doll who has been disciplined by your sweet little daughter.

unconscious How you'd like to be throughout your next pregnancy.

underground Where you bury dead pets that are too big to flush.

unrest What parents get when a child is sick.

urination What you spend half the day doing before childbirth and your baby spends half the day doing after childbirth.

utensils Tools that help baby propel her food farther.

uterus The tiny organ that stretches during pregnancy to the size of Yankee Stadium.

utopia That fictional wonderland where children say, "Yes, Mother, whatever you say."

vacuum The machine that sucks up small clunking items that are easier to write off than to recover.

vasectomy What most men find inconceivable.

verbal Able to whine in words.

veteran A person who has faced enemies in battle but is afraid to pick up a newborn baby.

vicarious The kind of thrill you feel when someone else gives birth to an eleven-pound baby.

V.I.P. Very Important Pipsqueak.

virus The disease your doctor claims your child has if he doesn't really know what's wrong.

visible Located where the baby can hide, break, or eat it.

visionary A person who can picture a toddler as a civilized adult.

visualization Picturing your family chatting amiably at the dinner table instead of fighting over the apple sauce.

vitamins Capsules that free parents from engaging in hand-to-hand combat to get their children to eat brussels sprouts.

warming dish How parents warmed the baby's food in the olden days before microwaves were invented.

wash-and-wear To shower and dress before your toddler commits a heinous crime.

water heater What your teenager fills with cold water by taking day-long showers.

weaker sex The kind you have after the kids have worn you out.

wealth What you gave up for the joys of child raising.

wear and tear What happens when children and clothes come in contact with each other.

wedlock A wrestling hold used by wives who want to get pregnant.

wet blanket What you find under the baby who's wearing leakproof diapers.

wet nurse A nurse who changes a diaper too slowly.

whining Mommy's home blood pressure test.

whiplash What you get when the baby in the backpack grabs onto a stationary object.

whistle-blower A child whose mommy has a headache.

white The color that should be outlawed in children's clothing.

whodunit None of the children who live at *your* house.

whoops An exclamation that translates roughly into "Get a sponge."

will What you can't threaten to cut your children out of until they're old enough to be materialistic.

window dressing An early indication that you're raising an exhibitionist.

wishful thinking Picturing your husband eight-and-a-half months pregnant and covered with spider veins.

working mother Any mother who gets out of bed.

worrier A synonym for parent.

xylophone The toy that provides children with a weapon to bonk out notes on other children's heads.

X-ray vision What you need when you think the baby has swallowed your loose change.

yard goods The items your toddler throws out the bedroom window at nap time.

yellow pages Any book a naked baby sits on.

yesterday What you hope today gives you a chance to recover from.

yesteryear The last time you got an uninterrupted night's sleep.

yogurt The baby's home facial kit.

zag What the kids do when you want them to zig.

zealot A mother who changes her child's clothes every time he gets dirty.

zebra The size a nursing mother wears.

zip code A hospital rule requiring all maternity patients to be fully dressed when checking out.

zits Teenagers' punishment for thinking they know more than their parents.

zoo The place where your child asks loud questions about the private parts of large mammals.

zzzzzz What you'll do soundly again when your children are grown and able to keep what they're really doing a secret from you.

Letters from a Pregnant Coward
by Joyce Armor

Here are hilarious letters of a terrified, over-anxious, headachy expectant mother, writing to parents, in-laws, siblings and friends. They express the fears and feelings that any woman who has ever been pregnant will recognize.

Order #1289

Grandma Knows Best, But No One Ever Listens!
by Mary McBride

Mary McBride instructs grandmas how to "scheme, lie, cheat, and threaten so they'll be thought of as sweet and darling." A great gift for grandma. "Harder to put down than a brand new grandchild." —Phyllis Diller

Order #4009

Mother Murphy's Law
by Bruce Lansky

The wit of Bombeck and the wisdom of Murphy are combined in this illustrated collection of 325 laws that detail the perils and pitfalls of parenthood.

Order #1149

David, We're Pregnant!
by Lynn Johnston
101 laughing-out-loud cartoons about the humorous side of having a baby by the creator of the "For Better or For Worse" comic strip.
Order #1049

Hi Mom! Hi Dad!
by Lynn Johnston
101 cartoons about the funny things that happen to new parents.
Order #1139

Do They Ever Grow Up?
by Lynn Johnston
A hilarious, 101-cartoon survival guide for parents of the tantrum and tears set.
Order #1089

Order Form

Qty	Title	Author	Order No.	Unit Cost	Total
	A Hundred Scoops of Ice Cream	Josefowitz, N.	2280	$3.95	
	David, We're Pregnant!	Johnston, L.	1049	$5.95	
	Dear Babysitter	Lansky, V.	1059	$8.95	
	Dictionary According to Mommy	Armor, J.	4110	$4.95	
	Don't Call Mommy	McBride, M.	4039	$4.95	
	Do They Ever Grow Up?	Johnston, L.	1089	$5.95	
	Grandma Knows Best	McBride, M.	4009	$4.95	
	Hi Mom! Hi Dad!	Johnston, L.	1139	$5.95	
	Letters from a Pregnant Coward	Armor, J.	1289	$6.95	
	Mother Murphy's Law	Lansky, B.	1149	$3.50	
	Papal Bull	Sullivan, D.	4060	$4.95	
	Playing Fast & Loose with Time & Space	Mueller, P.	4100	$4.95	
	Practical Parenting Tips	Lansky, V.	1179	$6.95	
				Subtotal	
				Shipping and Handling (see below)	
				MN residents add 6% sales tax	
				Total	

Meadowbrook Press

YES, please send me the books indicated above. Add $1.25 shipping and handling for the first book and $.50 for each additional book. Add $2.00 to total for books shipped to Canada. Overseas postage will be billed. Allow up to 4 weeks for delivery. Send check or money order payable to Meadowbrook Press. No cash or C.O.D.'s please. Quantity discounts available upon request. Prices subject to change without notice.

Send book(s) to:

Name ______________________________

Address ______________________________

City ____________________ State ______ Zip ____________

☐ Check enclosed for $____________, payable to Meadowbrook Press

☐ Charge to my credit card (for purchases of $10.00 or more only)

☐ Phone Orders call: (800)338-2232 (for purchases of $10.00 or more only)

Account # ____________________ Visa ☐ MasterCard ☐

Signature ____________________ Exp. date ____________

Meadowbrook Press, 18318 Minnetonka Boulevard, Deephaven, MN 55391
(612) 473-5400 Toll free (800) 338-2232